Getting Ahead in Maths

Getting Ahead in Maths

Michael Holt

Illustrated by Jon Davis

Longman

Longman Group UK Limited

*Longman House
Burnt Mill, Harlow, Essex CM20 2JE, England and
Associated Companies throughout the World*

© Michael Holt 1990
All rights reserved. No part of this publication may be reproduced, stored in a retrieval system, or transmitted in any form or by any means, electronic, mechanical, photocopying, recording or otherwise, without the prior writter permission of the copyright owner.

First published 1990
British Library Cataloguing in Publication Data
Holt, Michael
  Getting ahead in maths.
  I. Mathematics
  I. Title   II. Jon Davis

ISBN 0-582-06102-4

Set in 11/12pt Frutiger, 45 Linotron 202

*Produced by Longman Group (FE) Ltd
Printed in Hong Kong*

Contents

Number

Hundred square   9
Shopping with 10p   10
Shop-keeper's addition   11
Adding 2-figure numbers   11
Timesing   12
Short cut for adding   12
Adding squares puzzle   12
Thousands, hundreds, tens and ones   13
Mini times table   13
Four-, three- and two-figure numbers   14
Add and subtract up to 20   14
Halvings and quarterings   15
Fraction wall   15
Times table cloth   16
Times table square   17
Times snap   17
Square numbers   18
Matchstick squares   18
Division facts   18
Division snap   18
Estimating sums   19
Decimals   20
Percentages   21

Algebra

Odds and evens   23
What's in the box?   23
Input/output machines   24
Number patterns   26
Divisibility tests for 2, 5, 10   26
Doubling and halving fractions   27
Times table again   28
Area - simple formula   29
Prime numbers   29
First look at equations   32

Measure

Comparison of lengths   34
Standard measures   35
Clock time and the television   36
Estimates   36
Maps and scales   37
Areas of shapes   38
Volume of boxes   39
Guess how much it holds   40
Comparing weights   41
Handy conversion tables   41

Shape and space

Animal shapes   43
Sorting shapes   43
Shape spotting   44
Angles   44
Verticals, horizontals, parallels, perpendiculars   45
Making shapes   47
Making solid shapes   50
Tile patterns   51

Data handling

Book of number facts   53
Bar charts or block graphs   53
Carroll diagrams   53
Pictograms   54
Sorting by flow diagram   54
Pie charts   55
Temperature chart   55

5

A word in your ear

With the advent of the National Curriculum (N.C.), the maths children have to know and at what level is now unarguable. I have, accordingly, drawn from the curriculum key topics, arranged by N.C. levels, that you can most easily handle in the home with your child. I have adopted a simple style with a minimum of maths jargon, using just the basic technical words your child will need to know at school. The activities and games I've made up are all well within the scope of a junior school child and should not prove **too** taxing for a busy adult to cope with. Why, you may even enjoy playing them yourself – like dad playing with his child's toy trains!

Here follow some tricks of the trade for maintaining your child's interest without the need for heavy-handed coercion, which, in the long run, never works. Please, never make maths a punishment, like having to learn yards of poetry or writing out lines: that way your child will come, like so many of his or her forbears, to hate maths.

Try not to be too stern about correcting your child's efforts or it will become less than a game to him. Never make an issue of it. You could say for instance, "Hang on! You're sure that's right?" or, "Doesn't look quite right to me somehow." In other words, try not to play the heavy parent or old-fashioned teacher. Always be your child's best friend. If you feel confident, you could always pretend to make a mistake yourself and let him or her correct you. Children love correcting adults when they go wrong. They actually like you more for being human. For 'tis human to err. And if you do really make a mistake, for heaven's sake don't get upset or annoyed about it. Say something like, "Silly me! Thanks for pointing it out." and both of you feel good about it.

Try to look blank, like Buster Keaton, when your child is working something out, to avoid the most disastrous error of all: unwittingly encouraging him to look for the answer in your eyes or on your forehead. It is inside his or her head, tell him or her.

As your child learns, you do too. You learn the most valuable lesson of all – how to encourage your child to learn for himself. That, after all, is what education should be all about – how to give a child autonomy of thinking to think for himself.

umber

Number

Hundred square

zero → 0

1	2	3	4	5	6	7	8	9	10
11	12	13	14	15	16	17	18	19	20
21	22	23	24	25	26	27	28	29	30
31	32	33	34	35	36	37	38	39	40
41	42	43	44	45	46	47	48	49	50
51	52	53	54	55	56	57	58	59	60
61	62	63	64	65	66	67	68	69	70
71	72	73	74	75	76	77	78	79	80
81	82	83	84	85	86	87	88	89	90
91	92	93	94	95	96	97	98	99	100

You need:

- several sheets of large-squared maths paper
- crayons or felt pens

Give your child a 10 by 10 squared sheet and the felt pen. Ask him to write the numbers from 1 to 100, as shown here. Mention that zero (0) comes before 1.

1 Tell your child to find a number, 30 say, and ring it with a felt pen. Then ask him to find the answer to: 30 + 7. He should be able to ring the number 37 at a glance. Try several of the simple sums where he has to count on to the next row - such as 47 + 8 (= 55).

2 Tell him to ring any number, say 42, then to add 10 and ring the answer. The answer will be 52 in the next row, straight below 42. Try several 'add 10' sums.

31	32	33	34	35	36	37	38	39	40
41	42	43	44	45	46	47	48	49	50
51	52	53	54	55	56	57	58	59	60

Number

Shopping with 10p

You need:

- a pile of coins: 1p, 2p and 5p coins

Set up a 'shop' with things you think your child might like to 'buy'. Make up price tags for the goods, ranging from 1p to 9p, about half a dozen for a start. Give him a 10p coin and make sure he has plenty of small change.

1 Get your child to make out a 'shopping list' like this:

I buy	I give	My change is	I write
 7p (pencil)	 10p	  2p, 1p	10p − 7p = 3p

He wants, say, a pencil stub, price 7p. He gives you (or another child playing 'shop-keeper') either the exact money or a 10p coin, then he must say how much change he expects to get. He makes a note of the transaction, as above.

2 Place a 10p coin on the table and ask him to make up two lots of coins to the same total value (10p). Ask him to do this in as many ways as he can:

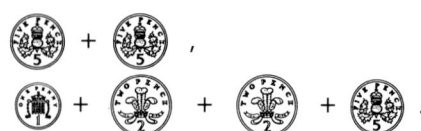

Number

Shop-keeper's addition

You need:

- price tags or slips of card
- several coins, 1p, 2p, 5p, 10p, 20p

Your child must find the correct coins to pay for some imaginary article (it can, of course, be real), its price clearly marked on its price tag.

Adding 2-figure numbers

You need:

- match-sticks or beads
- large sheet of paper with two columns drawn on it as shown below

Make up a sum like this one:

```
  35
+ 27
 ___
```

Now get your child to lay out matches in two columns on the 'mat', the sheet you play the game on. It is best to lay the matches out in fives, as shown.

Keep the top groups (*sets* is the 'posh' word) of matches separate from the bottom lot.

Now get your child to pull out any groups of ten matches that he can see, **from the Ones column**, leaving 2 matches in the **Ones** column. He must next move the group of 10 matches to the **Tens** column. This is what the 'carry 1' figure stands for in a written sum. Then he must add up all the tens in the **Tens** column. There are 5 tens already there, making 6 tens in all.

Written sum:

```
  3 5
+ 2 7
 ____
  6 2   (carry 1)
  1
```

Answer: 62 matches. It sound a lot longer reading about it than it actually takes to do in practice.

Now make up some sums yourself for your child to do. Make sure they all have 'carry 1's in them. Here are a few to start you off:

16	46	51
+ 64	+ 25	+ 19

37	47	52
+ 29	+ 28	+ 29

47	56	78
+ 18	+ 56	+ 19

Number

Timesing

You need:

- squared paper
- pencil, felt pen
- ruler

×	1	2	3	4	5	6	7	8	9	10
1	1	2	3	4	5	6	7	8	9	10
2		4	6	8	10	12	14	16	18	20
3			9	12	15	18	21	24	27	30
4				16	20	24	28	32	36	40
5					25	30	35	40	45	50
6						36	42	48	54	60
7							49	56	63	70
8								64	72	80
9									81	90
10										100

Mark out a big 10 x 10 square on the squared paper. Ask your child to fill in the squares with the times table facts. He only needs to fill in half the table (I have filled in the top 'half') plus the diagonal line of squares, 1, 4, 9, 16, . . . the *square numbers*. The other 'half' is the mirror image of the top 'half'. In short, the table is *symmetrical*. He can fill in the bottom half as well.

Short cut for adding

You need:

- matches
- paper and pencil

Here's a short cut for adding on 9 to practise, using matches or paper and pencil.

First add 10 then take away 1.

So: 43
    + 9
    ―――

Here's how he can do it:
43 + 10 = 53
Then he must say 53 – 1 = 52 Simple!

Make up some sums for him to do, like these:

  57   85   74   45
+ 9   + 9   + 9   + 9
―――   ―――   ―――   ―――

  28   16   33   17
+ 9   + 9   + 9   + 9
―――   ―――   ―――   ―――

Adding squares puzzle

He is a little puzzler for your child to try. Ask him to write any four numbers, up to two figures only, in a square which you have drawn out for him, like this:

30	7	
40	4	
		○

30	7	37
40	4	44
70	11	(81)

Number

Now he must add across and down to see if both totals come to the same answer, ringed in the bottom right hand corner. Your child can draw squares for himself and make up his own four numbers. Then you can check his answer – good practice for **your** mental arithmetic!

Thousands, hundreds, tens and ones

You need:

- several boxes of matches
- little cards, like visiting cards

Make up a board like this for your child to put matches on to represent numbers. Write out figures 0, 1, 2 up to 9 three times over, each on separate cards (visiting cards or filing cards cut in two).

Here is how to show the number 2063.

thousands	hundreds	tens	ones
1000's	100's	10's	1's
2	0	6	3
++++ ++++ ++++ ++++		++++	|||

Game 1

You lay out the matches to show the number you have thought of. Ask your child to put down the matching number cards. Get him to try this with several numbers.

There is no reason why your child should not make up his own numbers as well.

It could also be played as a game between two children.

Game 2

As a follow up, you could play the game the other way round. This time you lay out the cards and your child has to put down the matches in the correct columns to show the number you have laid out.

Mini times table

Look at this short times table.

Could you do the sum $\frac{12}{4}$?

You could, if you were smart enough to recall from your times tables that $3 \times 4 = 12$ or rather your child could. But you could also use this mini table to do the same job for you. No sweat!

$\frac{12}{4}$

×	1	2	3	4
1	1	2	3	4
2	2	4	6	8
3	3	6	9	12
4	4	8	12	16

Find the column headed 4, ringed in the table above. Look down that column until you come to 12. Then look left along that row till you come to the number in the left-hand column: 3.

So: $\frac{12}{4} = 3$

Number

Briefly, division is the *inverse* (opposite) of multiplication. Get your child to try out a few sums this way. To start you off here are a few such divisions:

$\frac{12}{3} = ?$ $\frac{8}{4} = ?$ $\frac{9}{3} = ?$ $\frac{16}{4} = ?$ $\frac{16}{8} = ?$

Now use the big 10 x 10 times table on page 12 and do the same thing. Here are some more divisions for your child to try.

$\frac{81}{9} = ?$ $\frac{72}{8} = ?$ $\frac{56}{9} = ?$ $\frac{63}{7} = ?$

$\frac{49}{7} = ?$ $\frac{60}{10} = ?$ $\frac{42}{7} = ?$ $\frac{42}{6} = ?$

$\frac{35}{5} = ?$ $\frac{32}{8} = ?$ $\frac{35}{7} = ?$ $\frac{27}{9} = ?$

Let your child invent a few of his own now. Don't press him if he gets bored, though. Let him come back to it in his own time – odd moments of practice are far more effective than a prolonged slog at the tables till both of you are heartily sick and tired of the sight and sound of them. Little and often is the golden rule.

Four-, three- and two-figure numbers

This is another game like the Thousands, hundreds, tens and ones game shown on page 13. Use the same board.

You need:

- plain cards or small oblongs of paper
- felt pen

On the cards write several four-figure, three-figure and two-figure numbers, such as:

| 402 | | 42 | | 4002 |

all beginning with 4 and having a 2 in them.

Ask your child to put the cards in numerical order, from left to right, smallest number on the left, biggest number on the right. So the cards should go:

| 42 | | 402 | | 4002 |

Now try these numbers in the same way:

| 307 | | 783 | | 873 | | 3078 |

Make up some more yourself or have him make some up and put them in order. Or he can test you!

You can also try numbers much closer together, such as:

49 and 51, 29 and 30, 58 and 61, 67 and 76

Add and subtract up to 20

You need:

- coins
- sheet of paper
- slips of paper

Put down a row of coins as shown on a large sheet of paper, ruled like this:

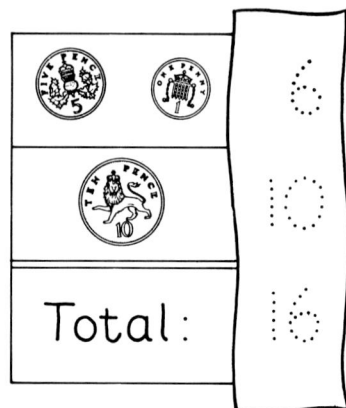

Number

Lay a slip of paper over the right column of answers. Your child can jot down his answers on it.

Ask him to add up the numbers on the right and work out the total as well. Do this for several different rows of coins.

Halvings and quarterings

You need:

- two lengths of string, about a metre long

1 Hand him one of the lengths of string. Ask him to double it over so that the double strand is half the length of the string. He can compare it with the unfolded string to check.

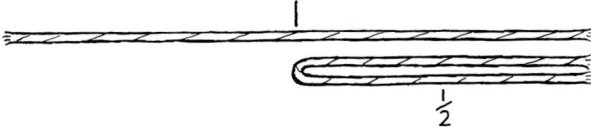

Now ask him to fold the doubled over length of string again to measure it against the original string to see that it is indeed a quarter its length.

2 Measure two lengths of string, each 8 cm long. Give one length to your child and ask him to double it over. He should now realise it is 4 cm long. He can check by holding up his folded string against the original string. And he should be able to work out that half of 8 is 4.

Now try with strings of lengths 10 cm, 12 cm, etc, all even numbers of cm long.

Fraction wall

Draw out this fraction wall on squared paper. Only mark in the numbers shown in **bold**. Ask him to fill in the other fractions. Each row is like the string he doubled and doubled again to get first half ($\frac{1}{2}$) then quarters ($\frac{1}{4}$s).

1				
$\frac{1}{2}$		$\frac{1}{2}$	
$\frac{1}{4}$	$\frac{1}{4}$	$\frac{1}{4}$	$\frac{1}{4}$

Now take a strip of paper the same length as the wall. Fold it over once to get halves. Ask him to mark the $\frac{1}{2}$s on the strip. Ask him to fold the strip double again, open it out and mark the fractions on it ($\frac{1}{4}$s).

Do the same, folding the strip in three to get thirds ($\frac{1}{3}$s).

Ask him to compare the $\frac{1}{2}$-strip with the $\frac{1}{4}$-strip to see that two quarters make a half. He can also see that two quarters make a half. He can also see that a third is more than a quarter and less than a half.

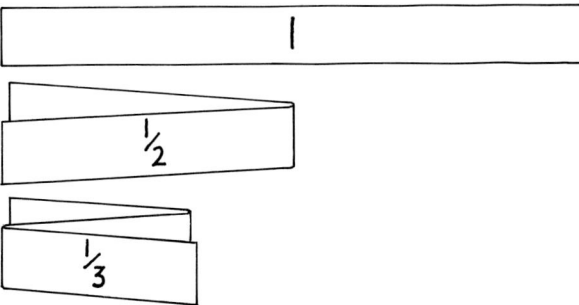

Number

Times table cloth

You need:

- several sheets of large-squared maths paper
- crayons or, better, high-lighter pens or 'See-Thru' markers
- black felt pen

Give your child a squared sheet and the felt pen. Ask him to draw a 5 by 5 square on the sheet and to number the little squares inside it with the numbers from 1 to 25. Also get him to make up another sheet with a 10 by 10 square and to fill in the numbers 1 to 100.

X	1	2	3	4	5
1	1	2	3	4	5
2	2	4	6	8	10
3	3	6	9	12	15
4	4	8	12	16	20
5	5	10	15	20	25

1. On the smaller square (1 to 25) ask your child to colour in first the 2 times table, then the 4 times table. He should see a gingham breakfast table cloth pattern begin to show. Explain that he should be able to continue the pattern without regard to the numbers after getting started. Observe how the pattern of the 2 times table fits into the pattern of the 4 times table.

2. On the sheet with the 10 by 10 square marked out, ask your child to colour in the 3 times table, the 6 times table and the 9 times table. The same gingham pattern should

X	1	2	3	4	5	6	7	8	9	10
1	1	2	3	4	5	6	7	8	9	10
2	2	4	6	8	10	12	14	16	18	20
3	3	6	9	12	15	18	21	24	27	30
4	4	8	12	16	20	24	28	32	36	40
5	5	10	15	20	25	30	35	40	45	50
6	6	12	18	24	30	36	42	48	54	60
7	7	14	21	28	35	42	49	56	63	70
8	8	16	24	32	40	48	56	64	72	80
9	9	18	27	36	45	54	63	72	81	90
10	10	20	30	40	50	60	70	80	90	100

appear. All the 3 times table numbers should fit inside the numbers of the 6 and 9 times tables.

3. On yet another sheet with a 10 by 10 square marked out on it, ask your child to colour in the 2, 4, 6, 8 and 10 times tables. He should get another gingham cloth pattern, with all the 2, 4, 6 and 8 times numbers fitting inside the 10 times numbers.

Number

Times table square

Mark out a big 10 x 10 squared paper like this:

x	1	2	3	4	5	6	7	8	9	10
1	1	2	3	4	5	6	7	8	9	10
2		4	6	8	10	12	14	16	18	20
3			9	12	15	18	21	24	27	30
4				16	20	24	28	32	36	40
5					25	30	35	40	45	50
6						36	42	48	54	60
7							49	56	63	70
8								64	72	80
9									81	90
10										100

Ask your child to fill in the times facts I've left blank. As you see, there's no need to learn the hundred times facts, only 55 of them plus those along the diagonal, making 65 in all. The numbers along the diagonal are called the *square numbers*, or *squares*.

Times snap

Make cards like these:

| 2 x 3 | | 7 x 7 | | 8 x 6 |

| 4 x 9 | | 0 x 0 |

and so on for all the times facts, making 65 cards in all. Now make out the answer cards – the products, as they say. For the cards below, they will be:

| 6 | | 49 | | 48 |

| 36 | | 0 |

The game is best played by two children. One player shuffles the pack of times facts and deals them out between the two players, while the other player deals out the cards.

Play starts with one or other player who deals a times fact card. The other player must put down the answer card – if he's got it. If he puts down the wrong answer card – here you may have to act as referee, or a third child can – the first player wins the 'trick' and picks up both cards on the table. If the second player hasn't got the right answer card, he puts down a wrong one, saying "Wrong" and both cards stay on the table. Play continues this way. The next winner picks up all the cards in the discard pile. The winner is the player who ends up with most of the cards.

17

Number

Square numbers

Get out the Times Table square (page 17) again. Here's a way to show your child how to make those square numbers along the diagonal. Get him to draw around the squares on a large sheet of squared paper like this:

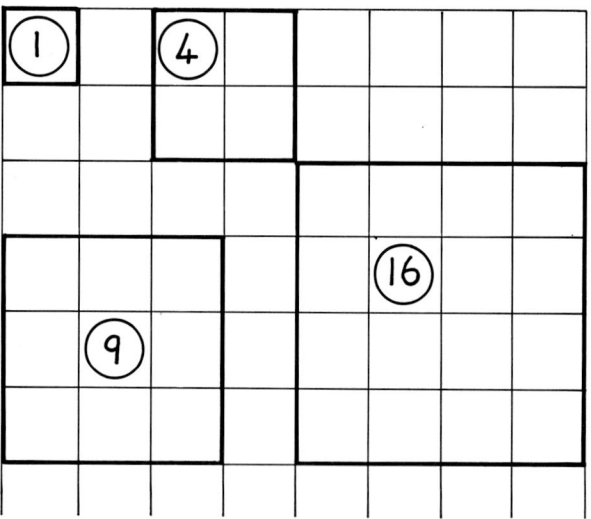

Put the total in the ring inside each square. The ringed totals are, of course, the *squares*.

Match-stick squares

Get your child to make the square numbers with match-sticks like this:

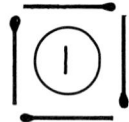 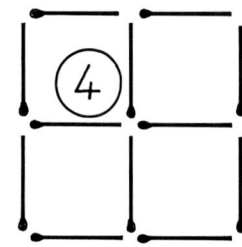

Division facts

×	1	2	3	4	5	6	7	8	9	10
1	1	2	3	4	5	6	7	8	9	10
2		4	6	8	10	12	14	16	18	20
3			9	12	15	18	21	24	27	30
4				16	20	24	28	32	36	40
5					25	30	35	40	45	50
6						36	42	48	54	60
7							49	56	63	70
8								64	72	80
9									81	90
10										100

The same method can be used for divisions on the big 10 x 10 table as you used on the Mini Times Table on page 13. You could ask questions such as:

$49 \div 7$ $56 \div 8$ $81 \div 9$

Find:

$100 \div 10$

Division snap

If you've got the energy you could make out cards as you did for Times Snap (see page 17) but with divisions on them. You will only need answer cards for the numbers from 1 to 10. Your child could then play a similar card game.

Number

Estimating sums

How many times in a shop or supermarket have you done a quick mental check of the total at the check-out? It's a useful skill to develop. Here are some 'wrinkles' for developing the same skill in your child.

What is, very roughly, 1472 + 383?

In your mind you say, '1500 and 400', rounding off to the nearest hundred. (They could be prices, £14.72 + £3.83.) So the total comes to about 1900 (or £19).

Try several such sums out on your child.

Now try a subtraction: 1472 − 383, the same numbers, you note.

Mentally you say, '1480 − 380', rounding off to the nearest ten (10). It is a matter of judgement whether you round off to the nearest hundred or the nearest ten. Answer: about 1100.

A paper-and-pencil check shows the true answer to be 1089 – only 11 out in 1000 which is about a 1% error: much more accurate than most banks work to, and certainly all governments are accountable by!

Give your child a few of these subtractions to do with paper and pencil or in his head. Have him check the accurate answer to see how near he could get by estimating or 'guestimating'. No harm in making an educated guess. A mark of intelligence, that!

19

Number

Decimals

Match decimals

Use the same board as you did for Thousands, hundreds, tens and ones (see page 13). Now rule an extra column on it, to the right. Head it 'tenths'. Lay out some matches as shown here.

	thousands	hundreds	tens	ones	tenths
	1000	100	10	1	1/10
matches			|||	||	⊞ ⁄ ||
numbers			3	2	7

(decimal point)

This is how we write 32 and 7/10.
We can also write it: 32·7.
Note the decimal point.

Set up some 'match' numbers, and see if your child can read them off.

Coin decimals

Now take some £1, 50p, 10p, 5p, 2p, and 1p coins. Put them down on a board like this one:

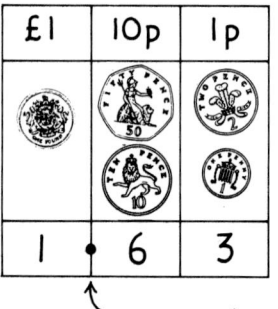

This line shows the sum of money £1·63.

Note the decimal point.

Set out several sets of coins and ask your child to jot down on a sheet of paper the sums. Tell him to put the decimal point between the pounds and the pence.

Number

Percentages

Simple percentages

The % sign means 'over a 100' or 'divide by a 100'.

So: 10 % means $\frac{10}{100} = \frac{1}{10}$

0% means $\frac{0}{100} = 0$

100% means $\frac{100}{100} = 1$

See if your child can quickly jot down a few percentages as you call them out. To make it easier give the questions as percentages of a sum of money. Thus:

10% of £10 = £10 x $\frac{10}{100}$ = £10 x $\frac{1}{10}$ = £1

10% of £1 = 100p x $\frac{10}{100}$ = 10p

And so on. This will sharpen up both your child's and your wits.

Coin game

Lay out some of your coins to show various sums of money. For example:

You ask: "What is 10% of each?" Your child must put down the correct coins.
 He could do it piecemeal like this, by taking 10% of each coin.

   = 7p

Or he could add them all up in his head and think 70p: 10% of 70p is 7p. The same answer. (It would be very unfortunate of it weren't!)

21

Algebra

Algebra

Odds and evens

You need:

- several counters – buttons, coins, beads
- large sheet of plain paper
- felt pen

Take a large pile of counters. Put them down on the paper in twos (pairs). Draw rings round the pairs. Don't count the counters! Count the rings drawn. Can you say how many counters there are? Play the game in pairs. The first players to get the correct total is the winner. Do this several times.

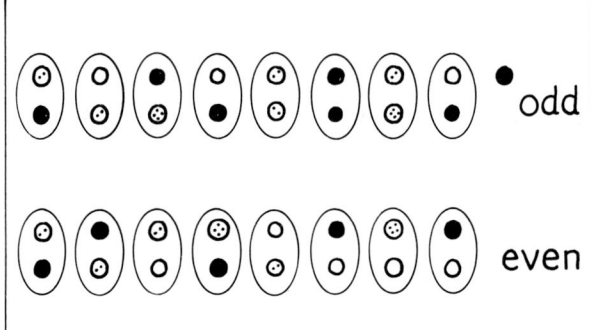

Now mix up the counters and add one counter. There must now be an odd number of them. Split the counters into two almost equal lots. See who has an odd number of counters again by putting two in each ring. The first player to get the total of the counters is the winner.

Take any number of counters. Put two in each ring. Suppose the number is odd. Do the same for a second lot of counters, so the total is also odd, that is, with one counter outside the rings. Put the two lots of counters together. See who knows if it will come out to an odd or an even total. (It should be even.)

What's in the box?

Make a card like this with a little flap.

Put down little cards with numbers on them like this:

Under the flap slide a card with the number on it.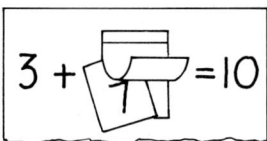

Ask your child to work out the number hidden under the flap. He can guess, or he can count on: 3, 4, 5, 6, 7, 8, 9, 10 – which needs 7 jumps to get from 3 to 10. Or he can take 3 off 10: 10 take away 3 is 7. When he's decided on his answer, he can lift the flap to check. All three methods should give the same answer. Try not to criticize your child if he guessed. Remember it is only a game. He'll get plenty of practice at school. Try to keep it light-hearted and fun. Don't make an issue of it. And if he gets the answer wrong don't correct him but ask him, "Why do you think that?" If he knows he's wrong, then you are winning, for half the skill in maths is to know **when** you've wrong, then to know **where** you've gone wrong and, finally, **how** to put the mistake right and get the **right answer**. So the rule is softly, softly. Try the above card game with lots of *equations* as they are called. Here are a few to start you off. It is also called *frame* arithmetic. The little boxes are called *frames*.

$4 + \square = 9$ $8 + \square = 10$
$2 + \square = 7$ $7 + \square = 10$
$3 + \square = 9$ $6 + \square = 11$

Algebra

Input/output machines

Make an input/output machine like this:

INPUT		OUTPUT
3	→	5
7	→	9
5	→	7

Game 1

Now, what is happening to the number on the left to get the number on the right? Obviously you add 2 to each number on the left.

So it is a '+2' machine.

Ask your child either to try '+2' or he can write it down on a blank card and place it by the machine.

Try other machines, such as +3, +5 or −1 machines.

Game 2

This time put down the card at the top and he must work out what the outputs are. I've put the answers for you in brakets.

INPUT	+2	OUTPUT
3	→	(5)
7	→	(9)
5	→	(7)

That is, you play the game the other way round.

Backwards machine

Take the same INPUT machine but this time make the arrows go the other way.

INPUT		OUTPUT
6	←	12
7	←	13
2	←	8

What do you have to do to the numbers on the right to get those on the left? From each one, you take away 6, don't you?

So you can see that taking away (subtraction) is the *inverse*, as they call it, of adding. Set up some more inverse machines for your child to puzzle over.

To start you off, here are a few, with answers, **not to be shown**, given in brackets above the arrows.

INPUT		OUTPUT
3	←(−5)	8
4	←(−3)	7
4	←(−7)	11

Algebra

Tandem machines

Put two machines together in tandem like this:

INPUT (+3)	OUTPUT
4	→ 7
8	→ 11
2	→ 5

INPUT (−1)	OUTPUT
7	→ 6
11	→ 10
5	→ 4

Don't show your child the answers '+3' and '−1' of course. Ask him to make a third machine that changes numbers on the far left to get the numbers on the far right of the pair of machines.

So he's got to make a machine that changes 4 → 6, 8 → 10, 2 → 4, etc. That is, a '+2' machine:

INPUT	+2	OUTPUT
4	→	6
8	→	10
2	→	4

Set up several more machines in tandem to see if he can find a single machine that does the same job.

Doubling machines

Here's another kind of machine, a 'doubler' not an 'adder' or a 'subtractor'. It doubles the

INPUT	OUTPUT
2	→ 4
6	→ 12
5	→ 10

number on the left, as you can see, to give those on the right.

Make up some 'doublers' for your child to try. Or get him to give **you** some to do!

Halving machine

You can make a halving machine with the same numbers, like this:

INPUT	OUTPUT
4	→ 2
12	→ 6
10	→ 5

Do you see something? It is really the 'doubling' machine working backwards. The number on the right is half ($\frac{1}{2}$) of each number on the left. A 'halver', then, is the *inverse* of a 'doubler'.

Get your child to see this by giving him several 'halvers' to try and match them up with the same numbers in a 'doubler'. Then he will begin to see that it doesn't matter what number

Algebra

is under the 'postage stamp', as it were: the result of doing a 'doubler' then a 'halver' is the same as leaving the number as it was. In other words, it is the same as multiplying it by 1. So briefly:

□ x 2 x ½ = □

Try several of these 'doublers' and 'halvers' with your child. And do let him return the compliment!

Number patterns

Number patterns at this level are really very simple.

Take the pattern 2, 4, 6, 8 . . . . What's the next number? It's the next **even** number, 10, isn't it? Or take 1, 3, 5, 7, 9, ... The next number is the next **odd** number, 11.

What about 5, 10, 15, 20 . . . . ? Well, they go up in 5's.

5 + 5 = 10
10 + 5 = 15
15 + 5 = 20

and so the next step is:

20 + 5 = 25

The next number in the pattern is 25.

Now you've got the gist of it, try out the number patterns below on your child for which I have supplied the answer and the pattern itself:

3, 6, 9, 12, ... (15; numbers go up in 3's: add 3 each time)

1, 5, 9, 13, ... (17; add 4 each time)

1, 3, 9, 27, ... (81; multiply by 3 each time)

1, 3, 7, 15, 31, ... (63; double and add 1 each time)

1, 4, 10, 22, 46, ... (94; add one and double each time)

Divisibility tests for 2, 5, 10

Is it divisible by 2?

There is a very easy way for checking whether a number is divisible by 2. See if it ends in an even number, i.e. 2, 4, 6, 8 or 0. Don't forget 0 as in 10 which is even. Thus 24356094 is divisible by 2 because it ends in an even number. Check if you like, or ask your child to, rather.

Give your child a string of numbers or ask him to invent them himself – as big as he likes. He can check if it is even by dividing it by 2 on his calculator – or with paper and pencil.

Think of a number: game 1

This is a little game to sharpen up your child's mental arithmetic. It sharpens up your wits, too!

You say: "Think of a number." (Say he thinks of 3.) Make it a single figure number to start with, so you can work the sum out easily.

Then say, "Double it." (He thinks: 2 x 3 = 6.) "Add 8." (He thinks: 6 + 8 = 14.) "And divide by 2." (He thinks: 14 ÷ 2 = 7.) "Don't tell me!" you say. "And your answer is 4 more than the number you thought of." (He thinks: 3, the number the first thought of, + 4 = 7.) He says: "Right! How did you do it?"

"Well, that would be telling," you say, adding slyly "Let's say I can read your mind."

Or you could say it's all done by algebra which he won't learn till a bit later on. That is how it works. You tell your child to double a number and add 8 to it then divide the lot by 2 which comes to the same thing as not doubling the number and adding 4. Simple when you know how.

Think of a numer: game 2

This time you say: "Think of a number bigger

26

Algebra

than 2." (He thinks of 7, say.) "Multiply it or 'times it' by 3." (7 x 3 = 21.) "Take away 6." (21 – 6 = 15.) "Divide the answer by 3." (15 ÷ 3 = 5.) "And your answer's 2 less than the number you first thought of!"

How does it work? Well, all you're doing is tripling a number and taking away 6, then taking a third of it all which is the same as the number you thought of less 2.

Is it divisible by 5?

Check to see if the number ends in a 0 or 5. That's all. Simplicity itself. Take 21375 or 50990 – both are bound to be divisible by 5. Check if you like or better still get your child to do so, either on his calculator or with paper and pencil.

Ask you child to dream up some numbers ending with a 0 or 5.

Throw in a few yourself that do **not** end in 0 or 5 – just to keep him on his toes, for they will **not** be divisible by 5.

Is it divisible by 10?

Even simpler than by 5. The number has to end in a 0. That's all there is to it. As you know when cancelling fractions like 60/30 you knock off the final zeros (0's). This is the same as dividing 'top and bottom' by 10.

Then $\frac{60}{30} = \frac{6\cancel{0}}{3\cancel{0}} = \frac{6}{3} = 2$

Give you child some numbers that end in 0 and some that do not. Or get him to think up some numbers – to check if they are indeed divisible by 10.

If a number is divisible by 10, will it be by 5 and 2? Well, yes, of course since, as you saw above, a number ending in a 0 is divisible by 5 and 2.

It also makes sense since a number divisible by 10 is divisible by 2 x 5 (=10), that is, it is divisible by 2 **and** by 5. Get your child to check this out on a few choice numbers – of your or his choosing. Children enjoy sorting out their own sums. They feel they are really on top of the subject when they're your partners in crime and not the 'subject' of your scrutiny.

Doubling and halving fractions

$\frac{1}{2} = \frac{2}{4} = \frac{4}{8} = \ldots ?$

What's the next fraction in the pattern? You

Algebra

find it by doubling the 'top' and 'bottom' of each fraction, like this:

2 x 4 = 8
2 x 8 = 16

And the rest is obvious:

$2 \times \frac{8}{2} \times 16 = \frac{16}{32}$

and so on and so on up to, say,

$\frac{512}{1024}$

Get your child to check that this fraction is indeed equal to $\frac{1}{2}$ (a half). Ask him to go further up the line, using a calculator if he likes.

So he can double and he can halve. To halve just read the pattern of fractions backwards:

$\frac{4}{8} = \frac{2}{4} = \frac{1}{2}$

Now try this pattern, by doubling:

$\frac{1}{3} = \frac{2}{6} = \frac{4}{12} = $ ... and so on.

Or reading backwards, by halving:

$\frac{8}{24} = \frac{4}{12} = = \frac{1}{3}$ ...

Try this pattern out:

$\frac{2}{3} = \frac{4}{6} = \frac{8}{12} = $ ...

And the next one is $\frac{16}{24}$, isn't it?

Reverse the row to do halving.

Have your child invent fractions of his own to try doubling. Then when he has gone far enough, he can try halving them.

Start with, say:

$\frac{3}{4} = \frac{6}{8} = $ ...

or $\frac{2}{5} = \frac{4}{10} = $ ...

or $\frac{3}{7} = \frac{6}{14} = $ ...

Times table again

You need:

- 2 boxes of matches

Here's our old friend the times table. Let's treat the multiplication tables to a new guise. Take some match-sticks. Make squares of them like this:

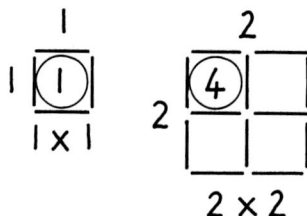

Then make squares for 3 x 3, 4 x 4, 5 x 5 ... if you have enough matches, 10 x 10.

Ask your child to count the number of single match-stick squares inside each big square he made. He should get the square numbers: 1, 4, 9, 25, 36, 49, 64, 81, 100.

Now try asking him to make oblongs – rectangles, if you prefer, though rectangles include both oblongs **and** squares! Like this:

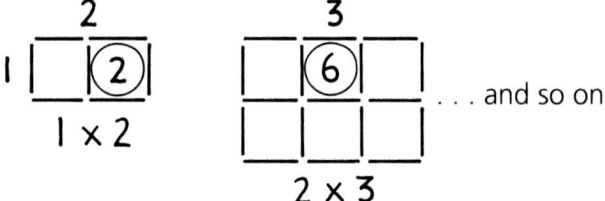

... and so on.

Ask your child to make up as many oblongs as he can think of up to 9 x 10, then count the 1 x 1 match-stick squares inside each oblong. For instance, inside a 7 x 5 oblong there are 7

Algebra

matches along and 5 down giving 35 matchstick squares in all.

That is, 7 x 5 = 5 x 7 = 35.

This game can be played in bits – never go on till your child gets bored. Let him stop when he's had enough or he'll not find the game fun any more. For what you don't find fun, you find hard to learn and harder still to understand. The great trick is to help your child understand – or **think for himself** with enjoyment.

Area – simple formula

Now we are going to use algebra on a simple problem – to find the area of a book's cover.

The area of a book's cover is the length x the width:

l = length
w = width

The area is given by the formula:

A = *l* x *w*

Not sure why? Well, think of those multiplication oblongs:

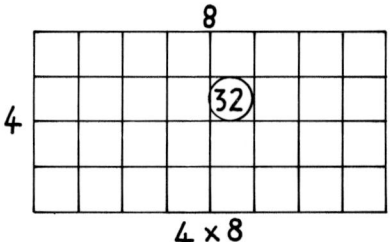

The answer to 8 x 4 is 32, got either by using your times tables or by counting squares. That's all there is to it, really.

So give your child some oblongs cut out of squared paper. Make sure the edges of your oblong coincide with the grid-lines of the paper. Ask your child to count the squares along the **length** of the oblong and along the **width** of it. Try several such oblongs on him. Ask him to one himself and work out its area by multiplying its length by its width.

Then ask him to measure the length and the width of the cover of one of his own books. Tell him to find the area of the book cover. Remember the answer will, of course, be in square centimetres (sq cm or cm²).

For this rectangle the area is 7 x 3 sq cm = 21 sq cm.

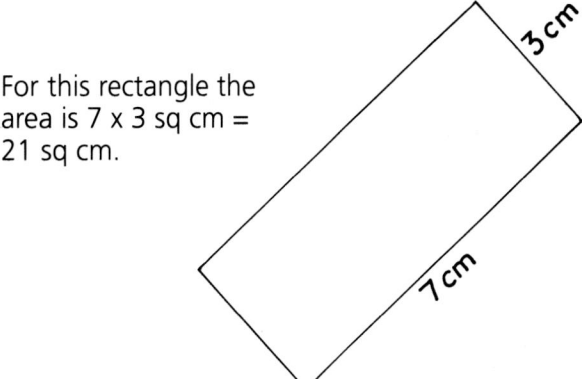

Prime numbers

In case you've forgotten or missed this lesson in your schooling let me remind you: A prime number is a whole number, greater than 1 and divisible only by itself and 1. However, 1 is not a prime number or 'prime'. 2 is a 'prime' because 2 is divisible only itself and 1 : 3 is for the same

29

Algebra

reason: and 5. But not 4 because you can divide it by itself, 4, 1, **and** 2. Every prime has only two divisors, remember, and the divisors must be different – which is why 1 is excluded: it is divisible by itself and 1 but they are they same number!

Prime game

Here's how to make primes into a game.
Make up this table for your child on squared or on any other paper you like –

1	2	3	4	5	6
7	8	9	10	11	12
13	14	15	16	17	18

and so on as far as you like.
By the way, most school books show a table that is set out like this:

1	2	3	4	5	6	7	8	9	10
11	12	13	14	15	16	17	18	19	20

It is called the Sieve of Eratosthenes – for sieving out primes. Eratosthenes was an Alexandrian Greek mathematician who lived around about 200 B.C. But my table is **much** more efficient. So I can't think why it is not more commonly used. Traditionally, tradition dies hard.

To return to my sieve, ask your child to complete it up to 50 or to 100. Now ask him to cross off all the numbers that are **not** prime.

prime rich columns
↓   ↓

1	2	3	4	5	6
7	8	9	10	11	12
13	14	15	16	17	18
19	20	21	22	23	24
25	26	27	28	29	30
31	32	33	34	35	36

You'll quickly see that nearly all the primes occur in the first and fifth columns, with none at all in the fourth and sixth columns and none, after 3, in the third because 9, 15, 21, 27 and 33 are all divisible by themselves, 1, and 3. But do not tell your child this – or you will blow the game for him! Let him find this out for himself. If he asks you because he's not 100% sure himself, you don't have to tell him that you know; just act a little dumb. "Probably", you can say, "Not sure. To be honest I'm a bit tired". And your child will be highly motivated to put you right! – a universal failing of human beings, I am afraid, which you can use to promote learning in your child. But for once, being put right will leave you with a positive glow of parental pride, **which on no account show**. Teaching maths is one part maths, three parts acting and six parts hard work. If you don't believe me, go in and try teaching a class of 30 unruly 7-year-olds. You will be glad you spend your days in an office, studio, laboratory, your home or wherever it is you work!

Algebra

Algebra

First look at equations

You say to your child: "Think of a number, double it, then add 2 and tell me the answer."
   What is his 'thought' number?
   Your child should jot down something like this (or he can work it out in his head):

   $\square \times 2 + 2 = 6$

   where $\square$ is his 'thought' number.

Now you can guess, almost 'see', the answer is 2.

   But how to work it out with harder numbers? Not so easy to see at a glance then. Here's how, using the above example.

   $\square \times 2 + 2 = 6$

This is an *equation*.

   Remember: What you do to one side of the equation you must also do to the other side.

To get rid of x 2 in $\square \times 2$, divide by 2

$$\frac{\square \times 2}{2} + \frac{2}{2} = \frac{6}{2}$$

You can cancel by 2

$$\frac{\square \times 2^1}{2^1} + \frac{2^1}{2^1} = \frac{6^3}{2^1}$$

Which gives you $\square + 1 = 3$

To find the value of $\square$ take 1 away from each side - so $\square = 2$

Try these out on your child. I purposely chose the numbers so that you stay in whole numbers all through the working with no fractions to upset anyone.

$\square \times 2 + 4 = 8$ (Ans: 2)
$\square \times 3 + 4 = 10$ (Ans: 2)
$\square \times 2 + 9 = 12$ (Ans: 3)
$\square \times 3 + 9 = 18$ (Ans: 3)
$\square \times 5 + 10 = 20$ (Ans: 2)
$\square \times 5 + 9 = 24$ (Ans: 3)

Measure

Measure

Comparison of lengths

The first step in measuring things is comparison – comparing the lengths of things.

Furniture removal – 1

Suppose you want to compare the length of a sofa with the height of a door frame to see if it will go through. You don't pick up the sofa, turn it on its end and move it to the doorway – unless it's some novel form of aerobics you're into! Well, suppose you haven't got a tape-measure handy, you can take a length of string and measure the sofa length with it and then offer the marked length of string up to the doorway. Get your child to do this to see if various pieces of furniture will go through the door. Remind him to check the width as well, of course!

An alternative: see if various objects, boxes, a fridge, a microwave, or the telly, will go through the window . . . using only the piece of string. Your child can cut off the required length of string each time or mark off lengths on the string with a felt pen.

Furniture removal – 2

Now get your child to play the same game measuring objects with his handspan or arm length (a cubit, as it is called in the Bible). He can also play it using tins or matchboxes to measure the lengths of table tops, fridge tops or the lengths of working surfaces in the kitchen.

Measure

Standard measures – length, weight, capacity

Now your child is ready to use standard measures. He can play the game, just described under Comparison of lengths, with a metre and centimetre rule or a tape measure; with weighing scales and with measuring jugs.

How much in a bottle?

Find some containers: milk bottles, empty tin cans (make sure these have no jagged edges for your child to cut himself on!), boxes, etc. Now fill each one in turn with dried peas or plastic beads or, in the Autumn, conkers or acorns.

Then he can tip the peas, acorns, etc, into a measuring jug to get an estimate of the capacity in cubic centimetres. Better still, but still messier, he can use water instead of peas, acorns, etc.

Measuring with string and tape

You need:

- length of string
- measuring tape or ruler
- Sellotape
- pen or pencil
- labels

Ask your child to use the tape measure to measure head, arm length, waist, hand span, length of foot of several different people: himself, his friends, you, say. On a scrap of paper or label, he should jot down the part of the body, length, in centimetres (cm), and, of course, the person's name. Then he can cut a length of string to the same length as each measure he has taken and fix the label to the

matching length of string with Sellotape. Then ask him to lay the lengths of string, side by side to compare everybody's arm length, say, and so on for the other parts of their bodies. The lengths of string should be put in order, from longest to shortest. The person with the longest arm length, say, wins the Longest Arm Game! And so on for the other parts of the body.

Ask your child to see if he can guess the height of the shortest and the tallest of his friends. Then he can check with their piece of string to see if he's right or how far out he was.

35

Measure

Clock time and the television

An old bug-bear with children, this one – though not such a big problem now with the invention of digital clocks.

Before and after

Before trying to teach your child to tell the time get him to grasp the difference between 'before' and 'after'. Ask: "Does tea-time come before or after lunch?" and so on. Since most children's lives these days are ruled by the telly, ask him, "Do you watch 'Neighbours' (say) before or after the 'News at Seven'?" And so on . . . till Close Down! Then try to teach the half hours, and quarter past and quarter to the hour. I should leave the problem of teaching the minutes to the school – unless you yourself feel particularly persistent. There is no hurry, though, to learn to tell the time – our society and particularly the telly is obsessed with time . . . and it doesn't seem to do us much good. The sun and the moon seem to carry on without a clock; so do our bodies if left to themselves.

We will look at time and television on page 55, in **Pie charts**.

Telling the time

The best way to teach your child to tell the time is to get hold of an old kitchen clock with a large face and large big and little hands. Then ask him to turn the hands to various times you call off. Start with the hours: 10 o'clock, 2 o'clock, and so on up to 12 o'clock. The 24-hour clock can be left until later.

Estimates

Guess the length of it

This is a valuable skill for all walks of life. How to estimate: the length of a sofa, or a car, or the width of a door or a window. Or indeed of anything.

Ask your child to guess any of these lengths; then check his guess by measuring with a tape measure. He must jot down his guess first **before** of course checking it out – or he may cheat against himself, which would defeat the object of the exercise.

Guess the weight of a cake

Just as at a village fête, ask your child to guess the weight of a cake you've made and jot his guess down in pounds or kilograms – it doesn't matter which unit he uses: the one he's used to. Then he can weigh it on the kitchen scales to check.

He can also guess, and check, the weight of his school bag or a plastic bag of conkers or a bag of washing up powder or salt or rice.

Measure

Maps and scales

Plan of his room

Get your child to measure the length and width of a room in your house – the simpler the shape to start with the better. Ask him to draw a plan of it. Obviously he will have to scale his plan down from the real room. Suggest he uses a scale of 1cm to 1m (metre). So a room might be 5 metres long and 3 metres wide. He can begin by measuring to the nearest whole metre. His plan of the room will be 5cm long by 3cm, like this:

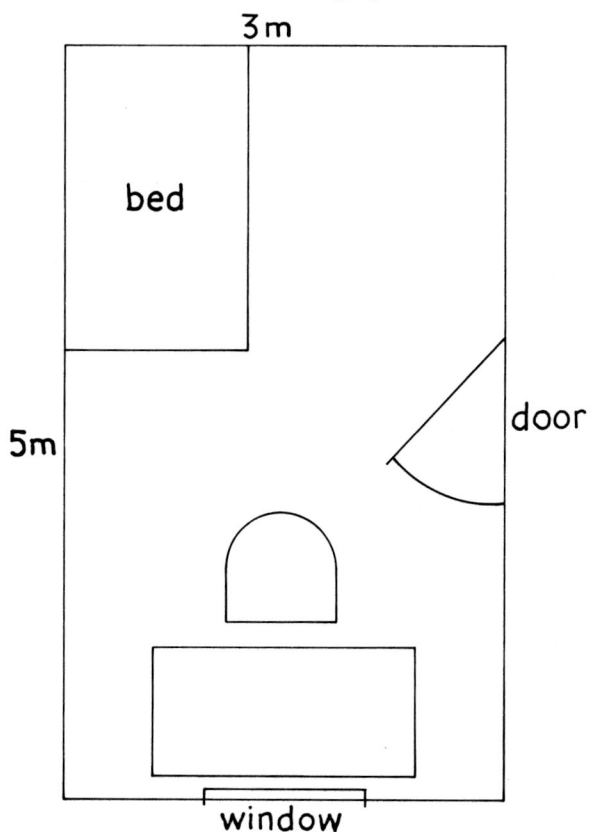

Map reading

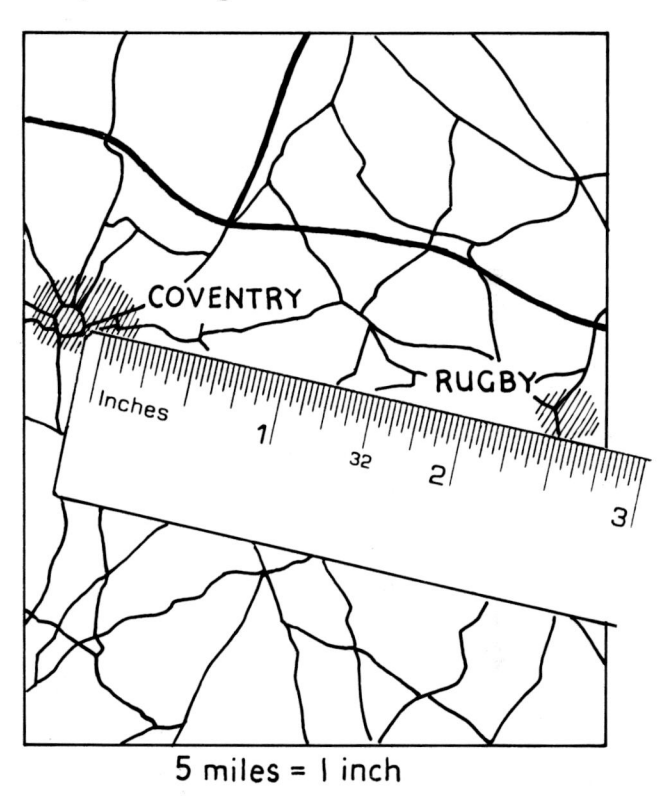

5 miles = 1 inch

You could get your child to read off the distances between towns he knows on a large scale car map, say 5 miles to the inch. He can lay his ruler along the map and read off in centimetres and millimetres (if he can handle the finer measure) the distance between, say Coventry and Rugby in a straight line. He must then look at the scale on the map. You can help him work out what the real distance is. If the scale is 5 miles to the inch, and Coventry and Rugby are $2\frac{1}{2}$ inches apart by ruler, the actual distance is $12\frac{1}{2}$ miles as the crow flies, or about 20km. Try lots of map reading games.

Measure

Areas of shapes

The area of a leaf

Tell your child to get hold of a large leaf. Now ask him to guess the area in square centimetres. This is a square centimetre:

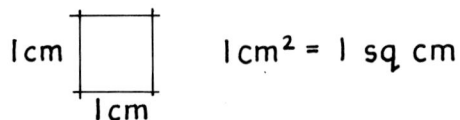

1 cm | 1 cm² = 1 sq cm

such as you get on squared paper. It is 1 cm long by 1 cm wide. It doesn't matter what size estimate he gives, so long as he makes a stab at it. If he doesn't, he won't be interested, still less will he be surprised at the answer he gets when he finds out.

Here's how to do it. Lay the leaf on squared paper with a 1 cm square grid. Now he can draw round the leaf with a soft pencil. His drawing may look like this:

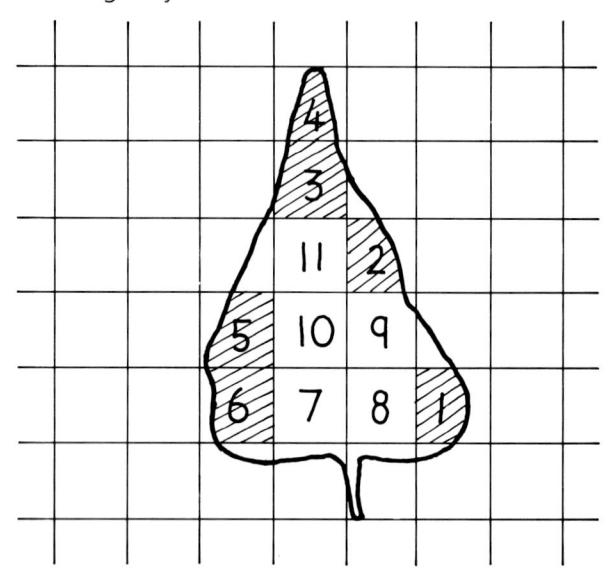

Next he must count the squares the leaf covers. Look where the edge of the leaf's outline covers part of a square. Count as a whole square if it covers half or more of the square – shown by the shaded squares on the sketch here. Where it is less than half a square, discount it. Then count up the squares covered by the leaf – in the sketch it is 6 shaded squares and 5 whole squares, making 11 squares in all.

So the area of the leaf is **about** (or 'approximately' as the textbooks say) 11 squares or 11 centimetres (sq cm or cm²). Get your child to try this on several leaves. Don't push it till he gets bored or you'll undo the good done.

Now get him to measure the area of a plate or a saucer by the same method.

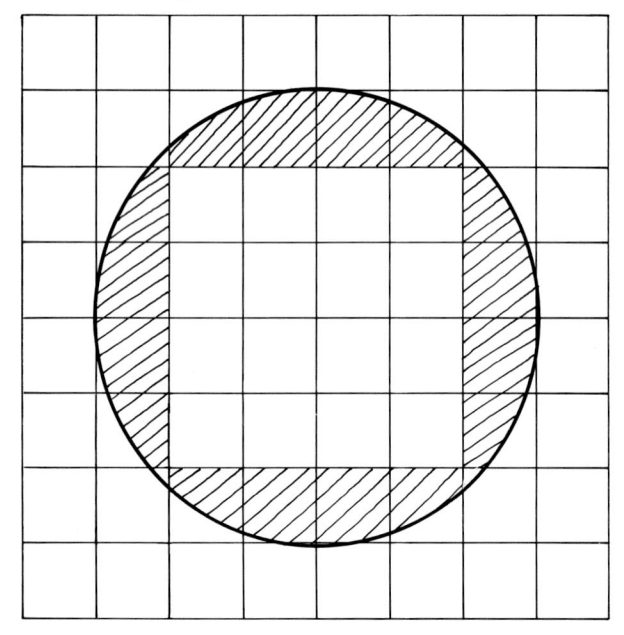

Measure

The area of an oblong

You need:

- squared paper
- pen

The area (**A**) of an oblong is its length (**l**) times its width (**w**). The formula for the area is:

A = **l** x **w**

Draw out an oblong on square paper.

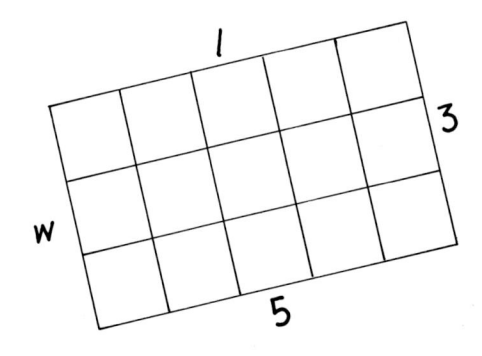

Make it, say, 5 squares long and 3 wide. Count the squares: 15, or you can use the formula with:

l = 5 and **w** = 3
A = 5 x 3 = 15 squares

Get your child to draw out several oblongs, which can include squares, remember – and see if he can use the formula to work out the area of each. Make sure he checks each area by counting squares as well.

Get him to measure the area of an oblong table mat in the same way. He can check this by measuring the length and width of the mat and multiplying the two lengths together.

Volumes of boxes

You need:

- several meat cubes
- sugar cubes

The **volume** of a box is

the length x the width x the depth

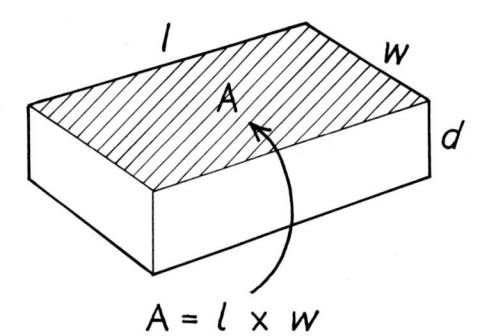

A = *l* x *w*

So: the volume (**V**) of the box is given by the formula:

V = **l** x **w** x **d** where **l** = length
                                                    w = width
                                                    d = depth

Why? Well, as we know from the last section the area of the top is **A** = **l** x **w**. Then, to get the volume, you multiply that area by the thickness or depth. That is:

V = **A** x **d**
     = **l** x **w** x **d**

Take the volume of a little cube, a meat cube, let's say. Its side is very nearly 2 cm (centimetres). So the volume of the meat cube is given by:

V = 2 cm x 2 cm x 2 cm
     = 2 x 2 x 2 cubic cm
     = 8 cubic cm

Measure

Ask your child to go through this calculation with you. Now take several meat cubes, 12 say, and make them into an oblong box like this:

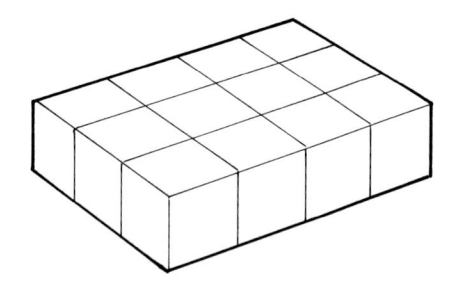

Give him a centimetre ruler and ask him to measure the box to the nearest cm. Obviously the top must be 4 cm by 6 cm. It is 4 cm deep. You can count the number of cubes (each 8 cubic cm in volume), so you can calculate the total volume of all 12 meat cubes: 12 x 8 cubic cm = 96 cubic cm. This offers good practice in doing the times tables! Now ask your child to work it out by the formula:

$V = l \times w \times d$
$V = 6 \times 4 \times 4$ cm = 96 cubic cm.

The same. It would be very unfortunate if it weren't!

Build up other boxes of meat cubes. Or you can use sugar cubes or plastic Unifix blocks. Again, assume a sugar cube has a side of 2 cm. You could use bigger cubes – children's wooden blocks, if you have any handy. And make sure you measure the side to the nearest whole number of centimetres.

Encourage your child to find other cubes – Lego, etc. – that he can fit together to make a box.

Finally, let him try to work out the volume of such box-like objects as a packet of butter (make sure it doesn't melt!), a box of tea-bags, a toothpaste tube box, a packet of soap powder, a cereal packet and like goods – in fact the volume of any box he can tackle – always remembering to round off to a whole number of centimetres for each length. That should keep him happy for quite some time – if it appeals to him. If not, go on to the next game.

Guess how much it holds

Ask your child to guess how much his mug or plastic beaker holds. (Better not let him get his hands on your glassware!) Now ask him to fill the mug, or beaker, with water and then to tip

Measure

the water into a measuring jug – without spilling a drop, if he **can**! Skill is required here. Then he can see how near his guess was. With practice he will get quite good at this – useful when he grows up and has to cook for himself! Or for someone else!!!

Comparing weights

Find the kitchen scales or bathroom scales. Get your child to compare the weights of various things on the scales. Get him first to compare the weights by holding them in his hands. Then to check his 'guestimate' by putting the things on the scales. He need not read off the numbers very accurately; just use the scales to compare weights.

Get him to compare the weights of, say, a cup of dried peas, a stone, a chunk of wood, a can of beans (or whatever), a packet of soap powder, a detergent bottle, or boxes of various kinds of breakfast cereal. Many of these commodities have the weight printed on them – the weight, of course, of the material inside, **not** including that of the container.

Handy conversion tables

Depending on what your scales are marked off in, here are some useful conversions that your child can learn by repeated use:

1 kg (kilogram) = 2lb (approx)
8 km (kilometres) = 5 miles, **exactly**
1 litre = $1\frac{3}{4}$ pints or, very roughly,
1 pint = $\frac{1}{2}$ litre

And to convert degrees Celsius (°C) to Fahrenheit (°F) use:

°F = 2 x °C + 30

Shape and space

Shape and space

Animal shapes

Get your child to make up some animals out of plasticine or play dough. It's best if they can be made up of **spheres** (balls), and **cylinders** (rods) and **cubes** (boxes). And some **cones**. Then ask him to make up some flat triangles, circles, and rectangles – that is squares and oblongs.

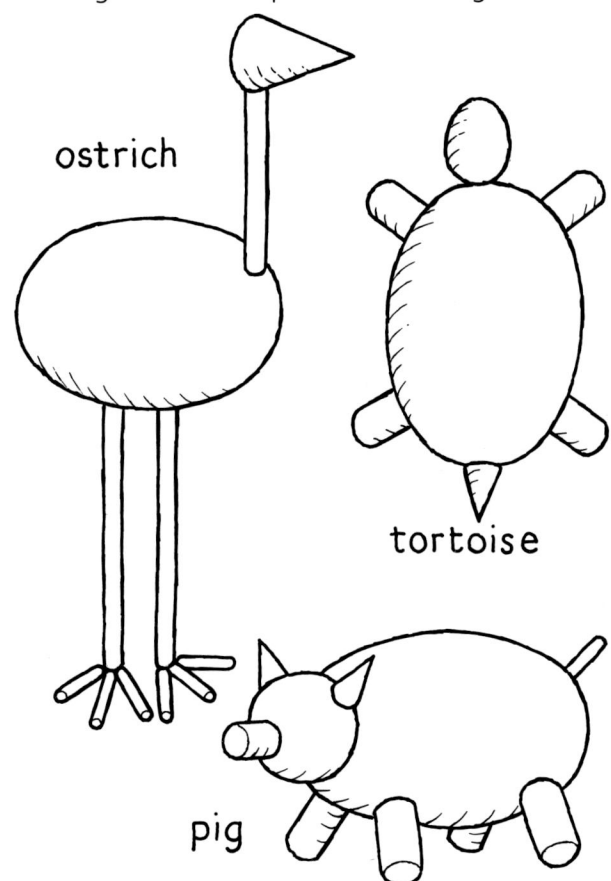

This is simply to give practice in getting to know the 'feel of' various solid and flat shapes. To get, as it were, the feel of space.

Sorting shapes

Find household objects, some with flat sides, some with bulgy sides, such as: boxes of tea-bags; a dog's ball; a vase (not too valuable or breakable, I hope); an eraser – preferably a rounded one and a box-shaped one; a round or oval bar of soap or a tablet of soap; a round pencil or felt pen (closed!) and a six-faced biro-type of ball point pen; pebbles; buttons.

Get your child to sort the shapes into two **sets** (groups) one of rounded faces and one of flat faces. Some shapes may have both rounded and flat faces. So they will belong to both sets. How do you sort the things shown below? Here is one way: you or your child can draw on a large sheet of paper, two overlapping rings as shown on the next page:

Shape and space

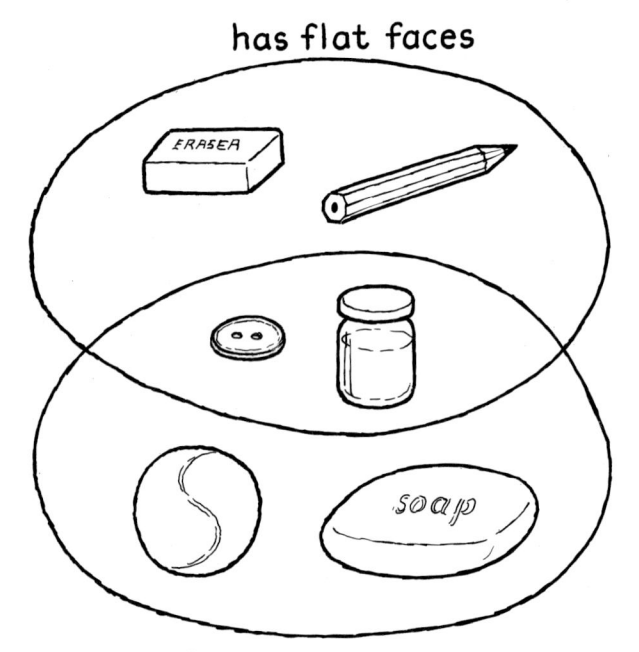

has flat faces

has rounded faces

This is called a **Venn diagram**. It's like a **Carroll diagram** really (see page 53). Now sort the same things into shapes with square corners and rounded corners, shapes with equal sides (like a pencil or biro) and shapes with unequal sides.

Shape spotting

This is a game to find shapes in the home. Get your child to look about and spot squares, triangles, oblongs and circles. It's a bit like train spotting. He can spot biscuits, box tops, tables, records, rubbers, rulers, paper plates, mugs, telly cabinets (not the screen because it has **rounded** corners), pencils, pens of all sorts and kinds, people's eyes and dog's and cat's eyes; cat's eyes on the road perhaps to be pointed out at speed only; rolls of Sellotape . . .

Angles

Right angles are square angles such as the corner of this page or of a ceiling, or a carpenter's square. A right angle is 90° (degrees).

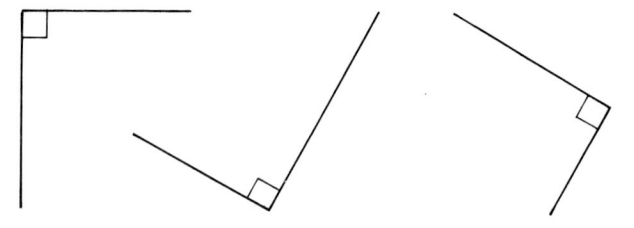

Acute angles are any angles *less* than a right angle, or less than 90°.

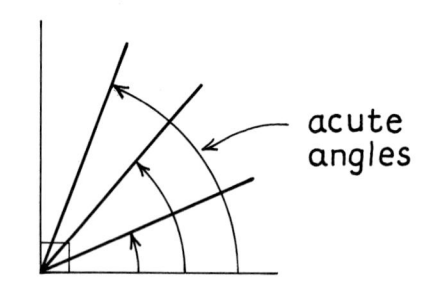

Obtuse angles are any angles *more* than a right angle and less than a straight line angle (180° to you).

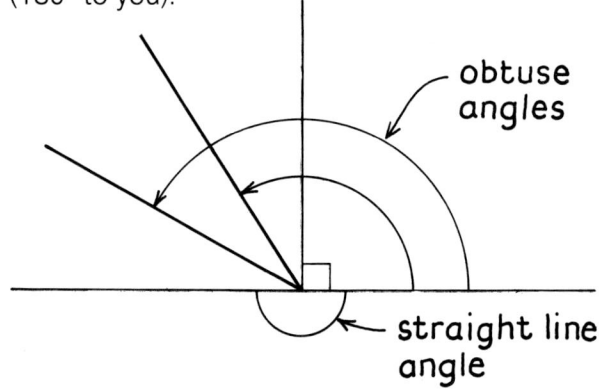

Shape and space

Don't bother your child with 90° or 180° yet awhile. He'll learn 'degrees' by degrees!

Reflex angles are angles more than a straight line angle:

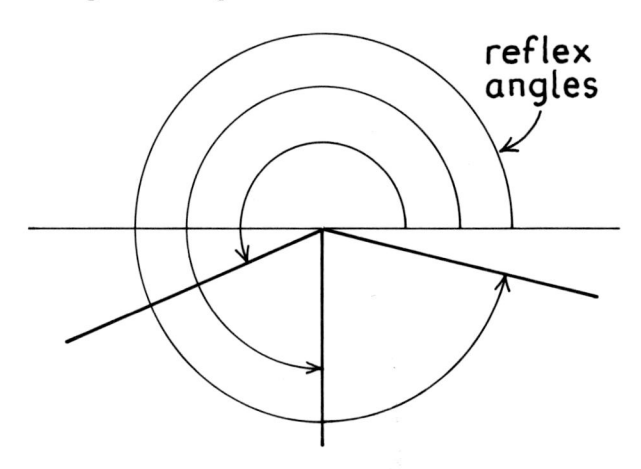

Angles on a clock face

You can point out these angles to your child on an old-fashioned clock face with hour and minute hands.

For a start ask him, "Is the angle between the hands when they show (say) 3.00 a right angle?" The angle round the back of the hands is, of course, reflex. You can pick out several of the angles he's learnt on a clock **and** tell the time at one stroke.

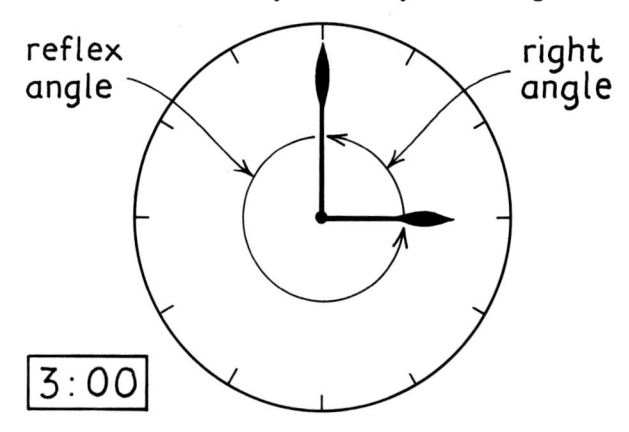

Verticals, horizontals, parallels, perpendiculars

Verticals are lines on faces of shapes. They go straight up and down. Point out these verticals: the corner of a vertical wall, the upright ends of a matchbox, a bread bin, a fridge door or the side of a microwave or a telly set.

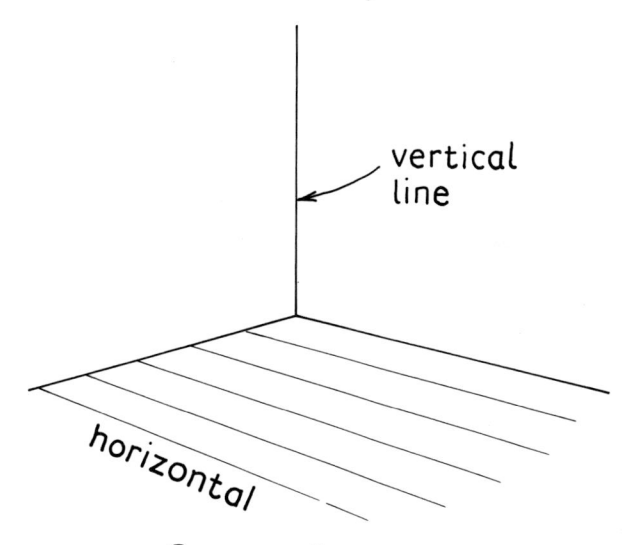

Corner of a room

Horizontals are lines that are on the level – on the flat. Point out these horizontals: the floor and the ceiling, a flat table top, the top of a matchbox, the working top in the kitchen, the surface of a mug of tea. The surface of water is always **level** as in a filled sink or basin, or a pond or lake.

Shape and space

Parallels are straight lines that never meet. Get your child to lay a ruler on a sheet of paper and rule two straight lines on either side of the ruler. The lines he has drawn are parallel. If they went on for ever, they would never meet. Other parallels you can point out are: railway lines, taut telegraph wires. High tension cables dip and so are not parallel. Point out parallel lines on this page (opposite edges). Look at the lines in an exercise book, or the edges of a matchbox. Verticals never meet; nor do horizontals.

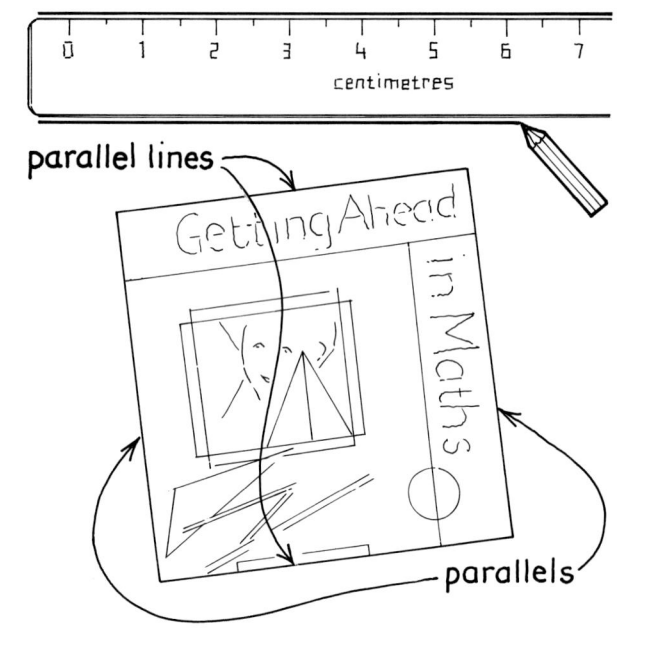

Perpendiculars are lines that are at right angles (90°) to each other. Point out various perpendiculars: corners of a room where the two walls meet such as a wall and the floor, a wall and the ceiling, or the next-door edges of this page. However, the lines **do not have to meet**. Take a meat cube or a cube of sugar. The edges shown **which do not meet** are still perpendiculars. Find perpendicular edges on a tetrahedron (see page 50).

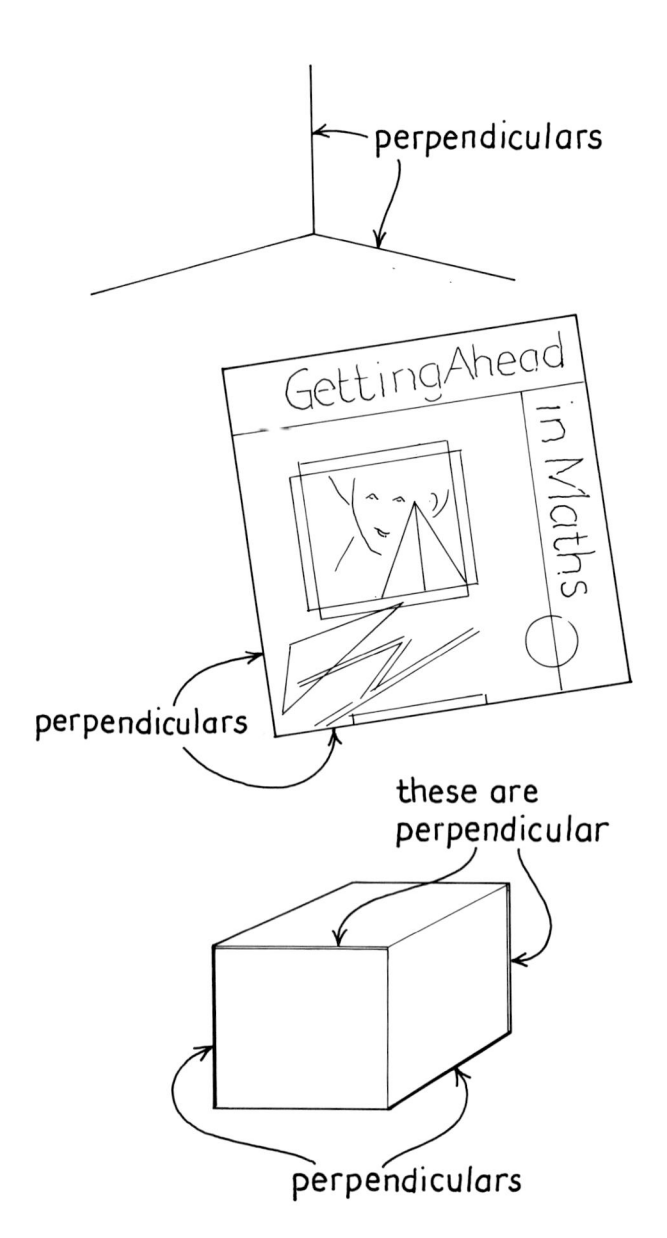

Shape and space

Making shapes – triangles, oblongs, circles

Here's how your child can make these shapes.

Single circle

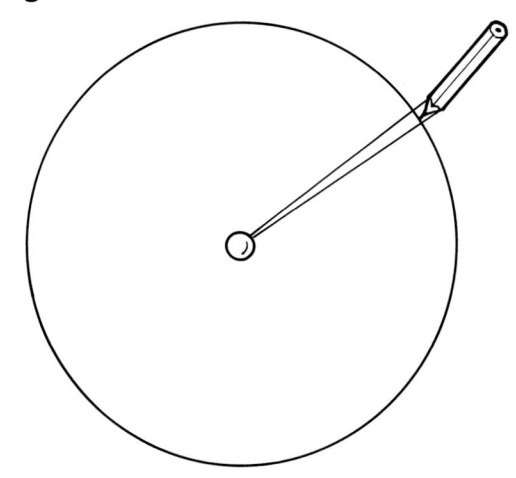

Put a drawing pin into a board upon which is laid a sheet of paper. Make a loop of thread. Fit one end of the loop round the drawing pin and round the other end fit a pencil's point. Now sweep the pencil round in a circle. Or you can get your child to use a compass, but make sure they are safe with it.

Triangle with equal sides

Get your child to do the following: Take out the drawing pin and put it anywhere on the circle. Draw another circle where the two circles cross over, put the drawing pin in and draw a third circle using the pin as centre. Actually, only a part of each circle need be drawn. The three circles overlap at three points, the pin prick holes left by the drawing pin. Join these points with ruled lines. The lines form a perfect equal-sided triangle – an *equilateral triangle*.

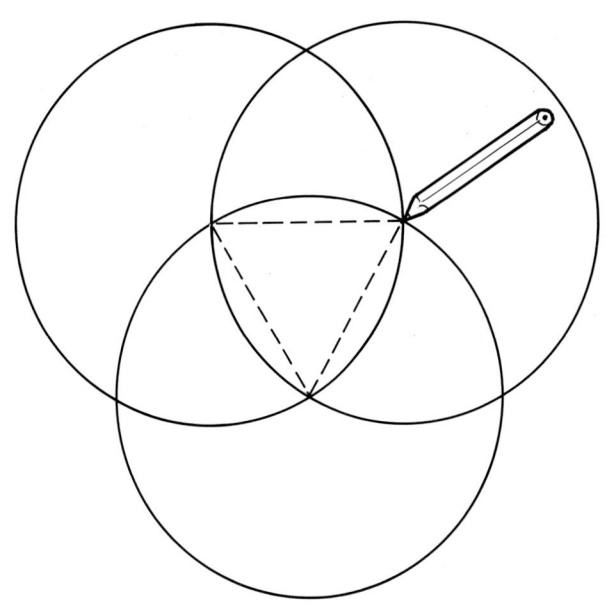

Drawing a square

Here's how your child can make a square. It's probably better to use compasses than a drawing pin and a loop of thread, though you could use that if your child felt inclined to.

1. Rule a line on paper.
   On it mark two points *A* and *B*, where you want the two corners of your square.

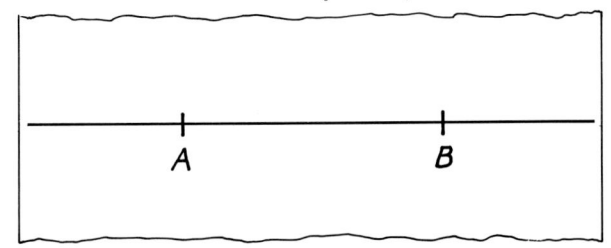

Shape and space

2 Put the compass point at **A** and swing the compass to make two marks on your line the same distance from **A**.

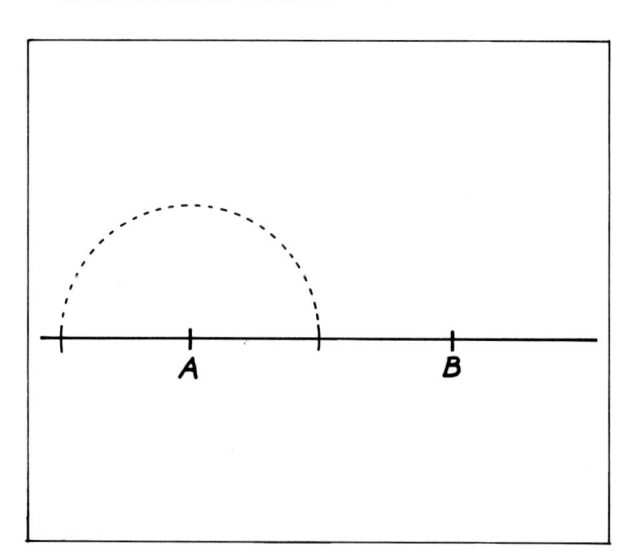

3 Place the compass point at one mark and draw a small arc above and below the line.

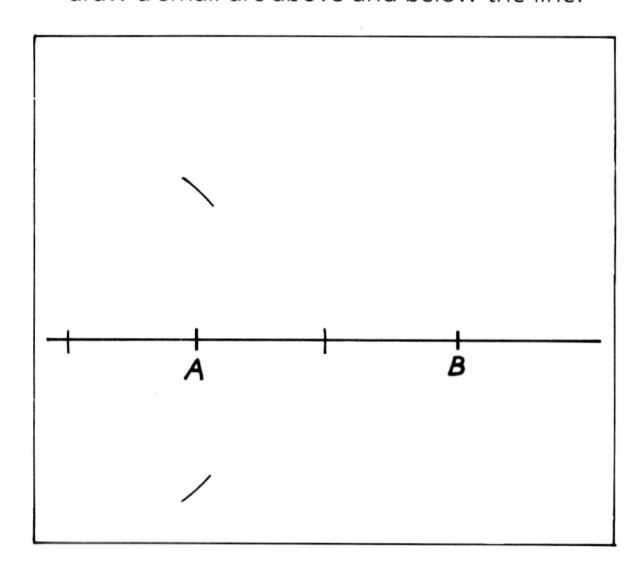

4 Now place your compass point on the other mark and draw arcs which cut the ones you've just made above and below the line.

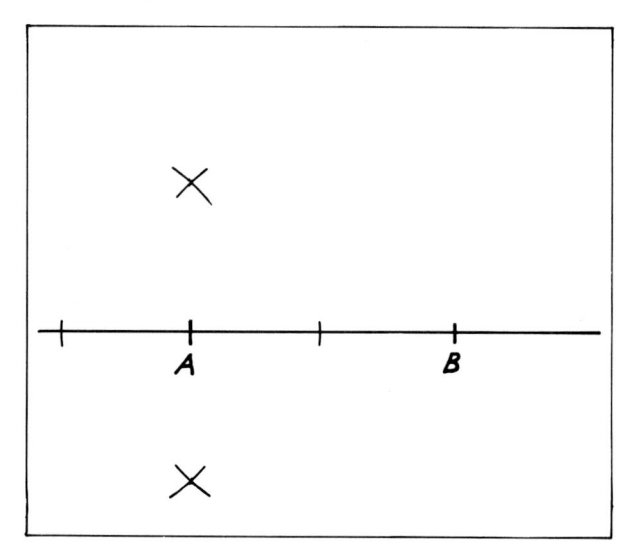

5 Rule a line through the crossed arcs to make a vertical line.

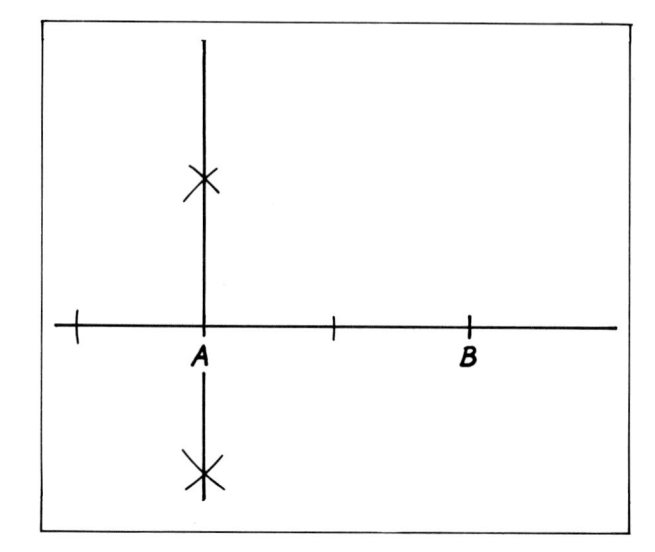

Shape and space

6 Now set the compasses to the length **AB** and swing the pencil to cut the perpendicular line that goes through **A**. Now you have a corner of the square.

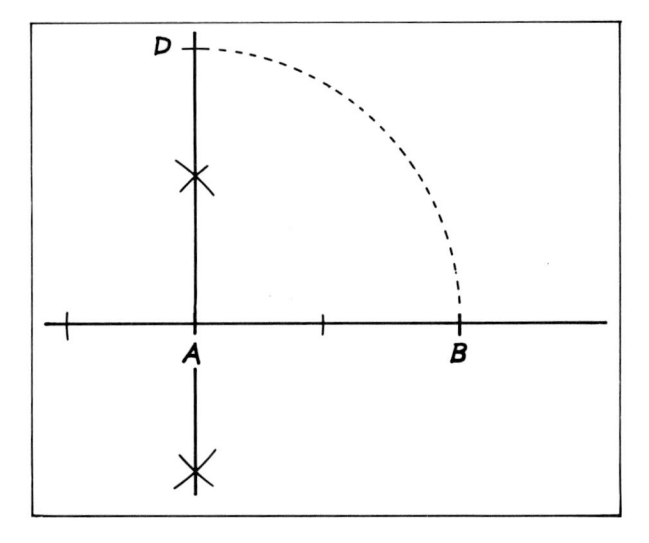

7 Repeat steps 2 to 6 at **B** to make the point **C**.

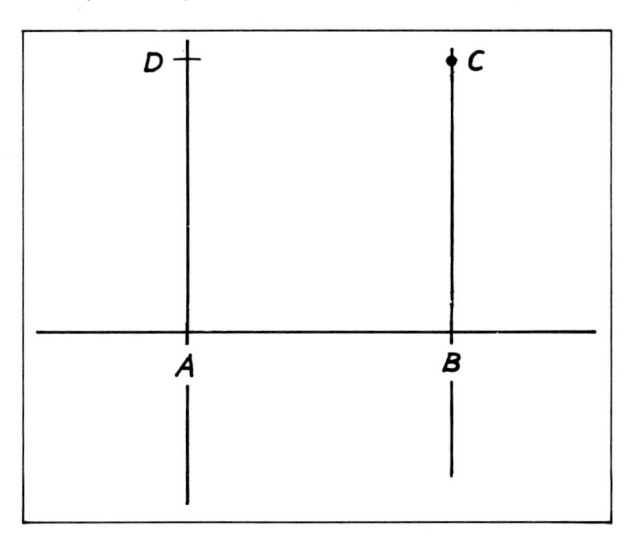

8 Join the two new points **C** and **D**.

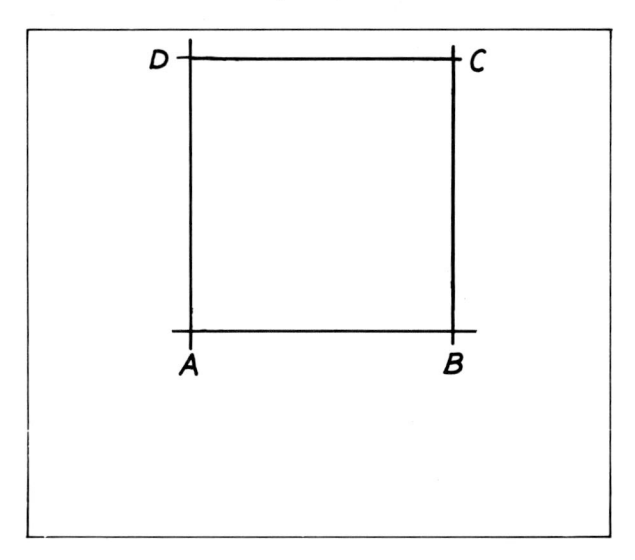

You now have a square, for the four sides are are equal in length.

Oblong

To make an oblong, you make **AD** and **BC** shorter than **AB** by setting the compasses to less than the length **AB** when drawing the perpendicular lines that goes through **A** and **B**.

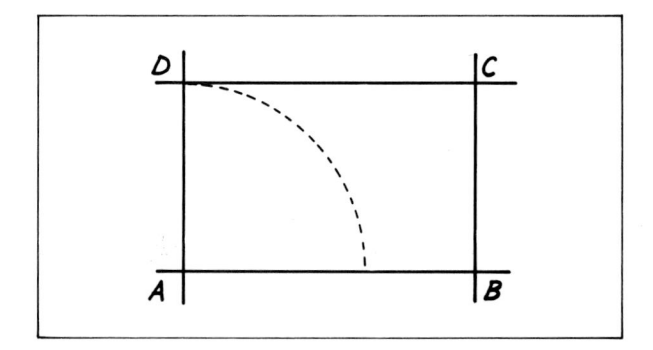

Shape and space

Making solid shapes

Net for a box

Help your child do this or show him how: open out the box containing 12 stock cubes. Cut off the flaps. You have what is called in schools a 'net' of an oblong box, or *cuboid*. It looks like this:

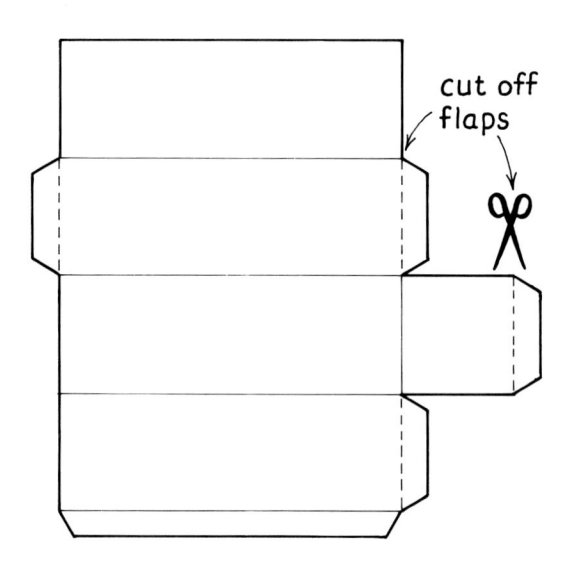

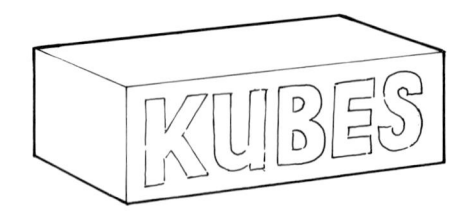

Fold it up again and you have a cuboid box. Note the two end faces are squares, all the four others are oblongs, all the same size.

Net for a firework

Make an equilateral (equal sided) triangle. See page 47 for the method.
 Mark the mid-point of each side. Join these points and you have made another equilateral triangle.

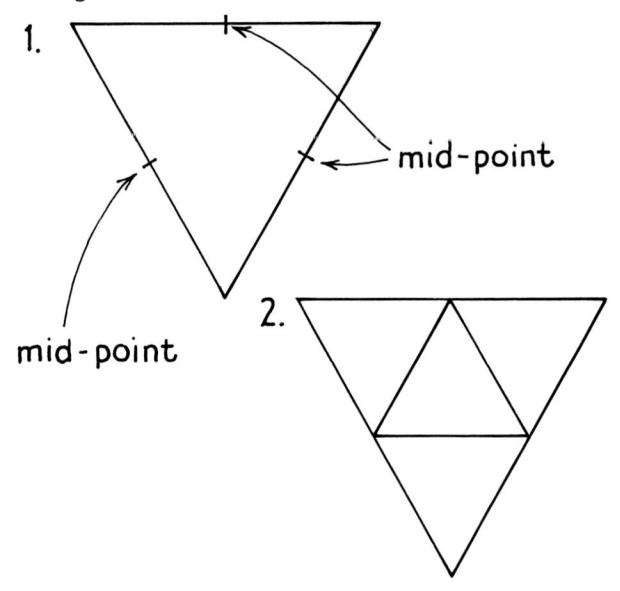

Crease the sides of the inner triangle or lightly score with the point of nail scissors. If your child is very young, supervise the use of scissors. Fold up the triangular 'wings' and join with Sellotape. You have made a triangular pyramid.

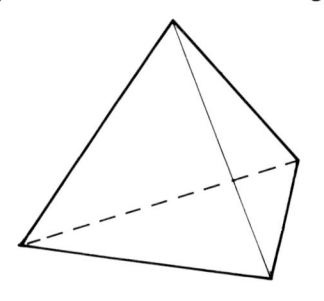

Shape and space

It's offical name is a *tetrahedron*, a Greek word where *tetra* means four and *hedron* means face. It is a 'four-facer'.

Ask your child to count the number of faces.

Ask him to find the edges that are perpendicular to each other. Not easy to see at once because the edges that are perpendiculars do not meet!

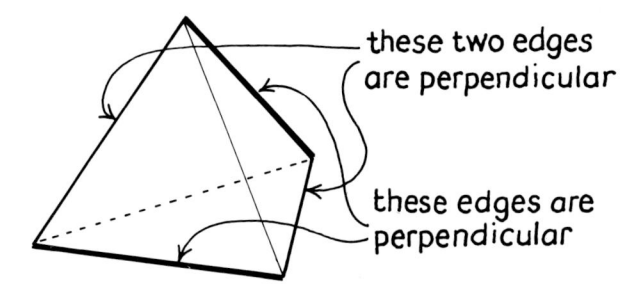

— these two edges are perpendicular

— these edges are perpendicular

The opposite edges are perpendicular to each other.

Get him to mark the faces. Get him to twiddle it round the point like this and see how many faces it passes through before the original face is facing him again (3). He can mark it with numbers and use it like a die or mark its faces with 1, 2, 3, and 4 spots.

Tile patterns

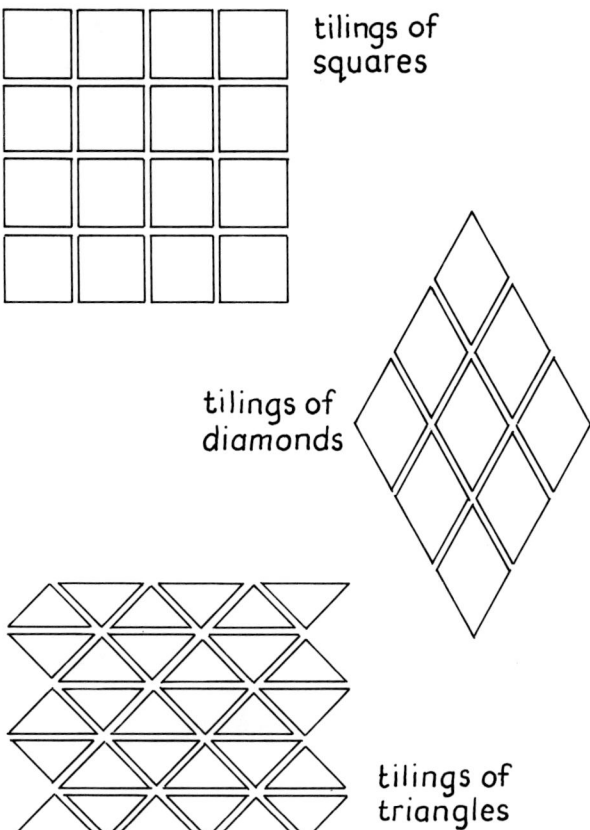

tilings of squares

tilings of diamonds

tilings of triangles

Square tiles on a bathroom wall or on the floor fit together to leave no gaps between the tiles. This pattern is called a *tesselation* in schools. You can also make tesselations (tiling patterns) with *equilateral* triangles – triangles with 3 equal sides. Get your child to find such tiling patterns about the house or in adverts in magazines. He can cut the ads out and label them 'Tilings of squares' or 'Tilings of triangles'. He can even try drawing them. He knows how to draw squares and triangles.

51

Data handling

Data handling

Book of number facts

You need:

- a big scrap book
- paste or glue
- scissors

Get your child to cut out number facts from newspapers (used) or magazines or leaflets, such as come in the post and stick the number facts (data) into a big scrap book. He can use such headings as:

- animal facts (speed, weight, how long they live)
- people facts (populations, etc.)
- car facts (top speeds, accelerations, lengths)
- shopping prices
- facts about the land
- facts about the sea
- travel facts (costs of air fares, train fares . . .)
- city facts (biggest city in each country, population . . .)

The facts can be used to make up the graphs which we show how to make later.

Bar charts or block graphs

There are many ways of sorting and handling *data* – figures and statistical facts gleaned from surveys.
    Your child will make these in schools. Here is typical one.

The way you go to school

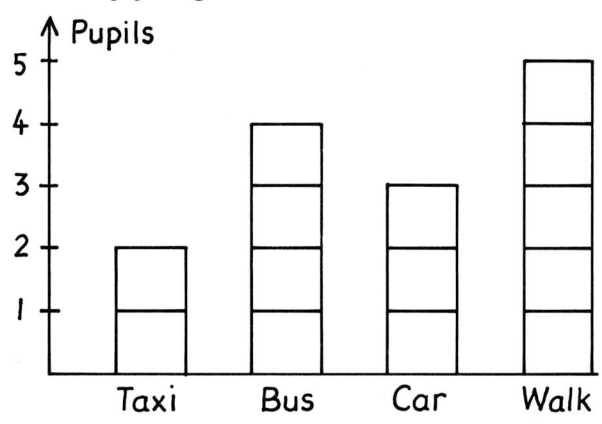

So it says 3 pupils in a class go by car to school; 4 by bus; 2 by taxi; and 5 walk there. Questions you can ask your child are:

Which is the commonest way to go to school? How many go that way?
(By walking: 5 walk there.)

Which is the least common way?
(By taxi; only 2 children go by taxi)

How many pupils are there altogether?
(3(car) + 4 (bus) + 2 (taxi) = 5 (walk)
= 14 pupils in all.)

Carroll diagrams

Here's a game you can play with your child.
    Collect some toys and household objects. Then sort them into colour and, say, texture ('feel'). So you might choose to sort all the **red** things and all the **rough** things out of some spoons, a doll, fluffy toys, sandpaper, nuts, apples, leaves and a hard brush – the bristles are rough, but the back is smooth! Problem: which is it, rough or smooth? Let your child decide.

Data handling

Now get him to draw the following diagram, it's called a Carroll diagram, invented by Lewis Carroll the author of the 'Alice' books. It has four oblong spaces for things to go into. Make it nice and big so he can put things like a few toys in each oblong. The lines do not have to be ruled.

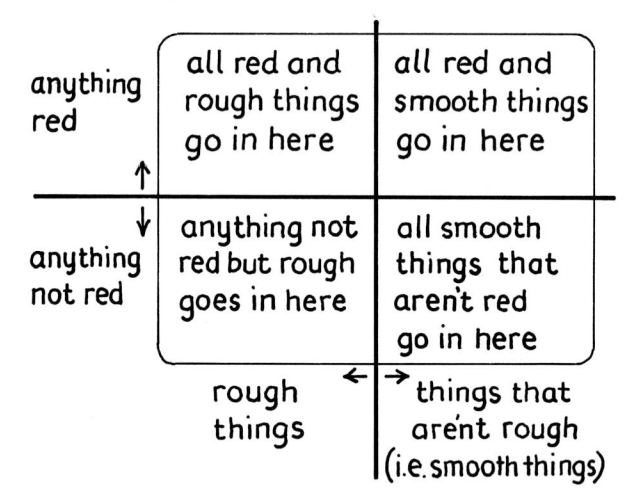

	all red and rough things go in here	all red and smooth things go in here
anything red ↑ ↓		
anything not red	anything not red but rough goes in here	all smooth things that aren't red go in here
	rough things ←	→ things that aren't rough (i.e. smooth things)

So we might end up with this:

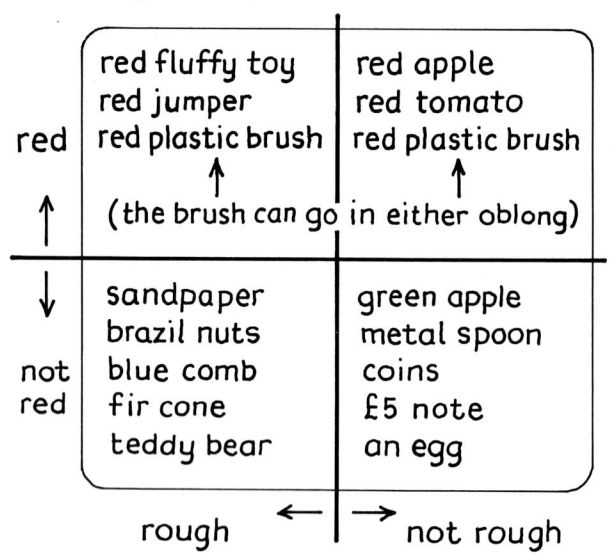

	red fluffy toy red jumper red plastic brush ↑	red apple red tomato red plastic brush ↑
red ↑ ↓	(the brush can go in either oblong)	
not red	sandpaper brazil nuts blue comb fir cone teddy bear	green apple metal spoon coins £5 note an egg
	rough ←	→ not rough

You could ask your child to draw Carroll diagrams of say: things that are green (or yellow) or rough; big or smooth; small or pointed; metal or plastic; and so on. Just choose two different 'qualities'. Good thinking for your child.

Pictograms

Your child will probably have done these in school. All you need to do is know what they are so you can help him with his homework. Here's a typical pictogram, or symbol graph. The number of raffle tickets sold by four groups of children at school.

(about 35)   Class A ■ ■ ■ ▪
    (30)   Class B ■ ■ ■
    (40)   Class C ■ ■ ■ ■
(about 45)   Class D ■ ■ ■ ■ ▪

■ means 10 tickets   ▪ = 5 tickets sold

Some questions you can ask:

How many tickets did Class A sell?
  (10 + 10 + 10 + 5 = 35)
Which class sold the most tickets? (Class D)
Which sold the least? (Class B)
How many more tickets did Class D sell than
  Class A? (45 - 35 = 10)
Did any two classes sell the same number of
  tickets? (No)
How many tickets were sold altogether?
  (35 + 30 + 40 + 45 = 150)

Sorting by flow diagram

Here is another way of sorting those toys and things you or your child gathered for the Carroll diagram. This is called a flow diagram. It is the way a very crude computer sorts numbers.

Data handling

Draw out the frame on a large sheet of paper. Make up cards on which you write to go in the diagonals.

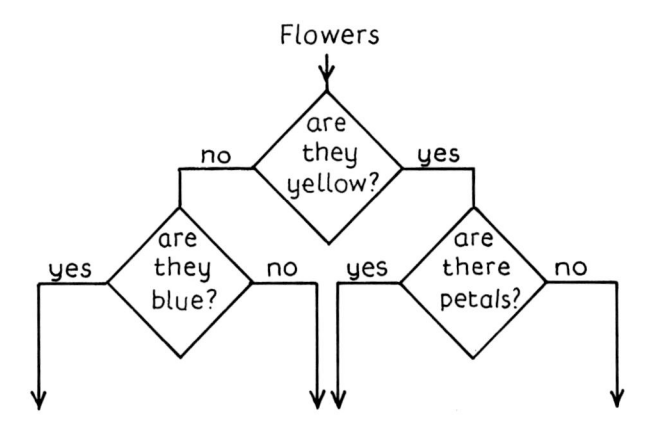

```
              Flowers
                 ↓
              are
         no  they  yes
             yellow?
      are              are
  yes they  no   yes  there  no
     blue?            petals?
   ↓        ↓ ↓               ↓
```

You can make up other cards, such as:

Is it a flower?   Is it yellow?   Is it big?
Is it smooth?   Is it plastic?   Is it heavy?

Pie charts

Your child will make plenty of these at school. So this is just to show you what one is in case he needs extra practice at home.

Here is a pie chart of how a young child might spend his day:

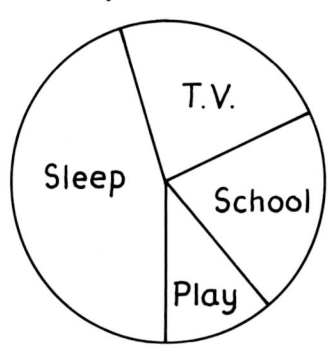

You can ask your child questions about the pie chart, like:

Which does Sophie (or James) do most of? (sleeping)
Which least of? (playing)

Temperature chart

Get your child to take the temperature on a thermometer hanging on a wall outside. Then make a table of temperature and hours of day.

Time	09a.m.	10a.m.	11a.m.	12a.m.	13p.m.
Temp.	15°C	17°C	18°C	18°C	17°C

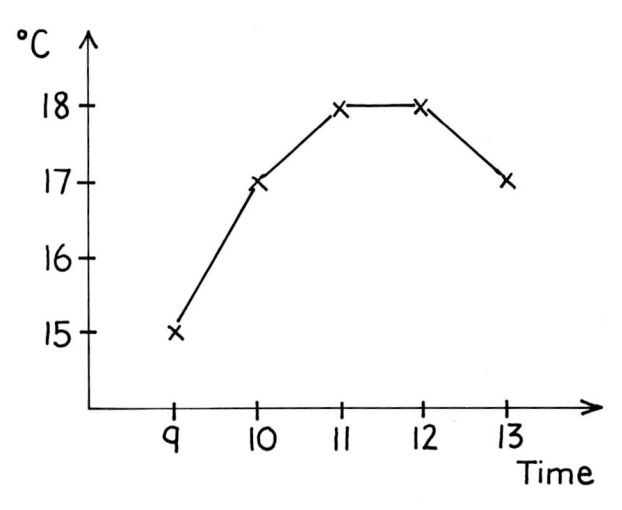

Then he can mark a cross for the temperature on a graph, for the various times. Then he can join the crosses with straight lines. This gives a temperature chart. The values in between the crosses are not real – they are 'smoothed out' values.

55